# ALISON HOLST'S BEST BAKING

*Alison's most popular baking made even quicker & easier*

## BY SIMON AND ALISON HOLST

Published by Hyndman Publishing
P.O. Box 5017, Dunedin
ISBN 1-877168-23-8

© TEXT: Simon & Alison Holst

DESIGNER: Rob Di Leva

PHOTOGRAPHER: Lindsay Keats

ILLUSTRATION: Clare Ferguson

HOME ECONOMISTS: Simon & Alison Holst,
Jane Ritchie

PRINTING: Tablet Colour Print

3rd Reprint April 2005

The recipes in this book have been carefully tested
by the authors. The publisher and the authors have
made every effort to ensure that the instructions are
accurate and safe, but they cannot accept liability for
any resulting injury or loss or damage to property
whether direct or consequential.

Because ovens and microwave ovens vary so much,
you should take the cooking times suggested in
recipes as guides only. The first time you make a
recipe, check it at intervals to make sure it is not
cooking faster, or more slowly than expected.

Always follow the detailed instructions given by
manufacturers of your appliances and equipment,
rather than the more general instructions given in
these recipes.

# Contents

**COVER SHOT:** Apricot & Almond Cake (centre),
Left to Right, Easy Oaty Cookies (page 16),
Butterscotch Fingers (page 55), Coconut Whiskers
(page 28), Cherry Slice (page 56), Custard Kisses
(page 13) and Peanut Plus Cookies (page 15)

*For muffins, a selection of Christmas
cakes and other Christmas baking, see
other books in this series (back cover).*

# About this book

What does "baking" mean to you?

To me, it means the welcoming warmth of a busy kitchen, with the inviting aromas of butter, spices, vanilla, and eggs greeting me as I open the door! In my mind's eye, I see my mother, flushed, somewhat dishevelled, surrounded by baking.

Once a week she would make enough to add two different items to four packed lunches five days a week, provide treats for friends who dropped in, for after-school snacks, and for suppertime goodies to enjoy with my father after we were tucked into bed.

This weekly baking did not include the four or so batches of hot scones or pikelets, "whipped up" a couple of times each day at the weekend. These were served mid-morning and mid-afternoon, between our varied sporting activities, walks, visits to the library, and churchgoing, and were also taken on picnics.

As well, my mother always found time to bake something to welcome a new neighbour, take to someone who was ill, fill the tins of a young mother with a new baby, provide an occasional treat for the local school teachers' morning teas, help the vicar's wife feed parishioners who came to talk to her husband, or thank a friend for a favour. She would take a "plate" to Mothers' Union meetings, leave a surprise in the milkbox for the milkman's young helper, and offer "a little something" to the postman or delivery boys, if they seemed tired, or if the day was wet and miserable. If there was a "Bring and Buy Sale" for our school, church, or any other worthy organisation, my mother would send us running along as delivery girls, bearing at least a dozen contributions.

Perhaps my mother's "best baking" was reserved for her formal afternoon tea parties, when half a dozen "staff wives" would arrive, by tram or bus, to sit in front of the fire beside a bouquet of garden flowers in our "sitting room". A groaning tea wagon, containing eight or nine of my mother's specialties, would be wheeled in! I don't remember the occasion when as a toddler, I jumped on to the wagon amongst the cakes, but I certainly remember the three of us waiting impatiently for the time when that tea wagon would be wheeled out again so we could eat the leftovers while my mother was still busy with her guests.

On regular holidays to the farms of friends or relations, my mother, a farm girl herself, was in her element. The two women "baked up a storm" between three cooked meals every day, turning farm-fresh butter, eggs and cream into mouthwatering morning and afternoon teas, not only for the farm workers, but for the dozen or so members of two families (and any passing visitors) who waited expectantly on the wide and shady verandah at 10am and 3pm, for hot scones, pikelets, gingerbread and cream-filled sponge drops.

I feel exhausted even writing about this! How could I ever have felt that my mother, a wonderfully warm, helpful and outgoing woman, must have time on her hands, and how can I consider myself a baker at all, feeling pleased with myself if I have one or two home-baked items in my pantry or freezer!

Times change, however. My family's

# *About this book* (continued)

present life-style is most certainly different from mine as a child. We are not nearly as active, so we need much less food. I give emphasis to smaller, more highly seasoned and more varied meals than those I ate as a child, but I still feel that there is a place for home-baking, which I prefer to bought sweets, chocolate bars, and packaged biscuits and cakes which are sometimes disappointing as well as expensive.

For me, baking is closely associated with family pleasures. I am overwhelmed when my daughter bakes me a basket of the little cheesecake tarts which my mother taught her to cook when she was four years old, or includes a jar of his mother's rock cakes in a birthday present for my husband. I bake at a low table in my kitchen with granddaughters who produce very creditable results, and pass them round with justifiable pride. In days gone by I encouraged my son (then a reluctant reader) to read recipes, so he could cook his favourite biscuits, and I am quite taken aback when he now says, in a shocked tone, "We can't POSSIBLY leave this recipe out, even if it is a bit fussy – I'll just simplify it", and I love it when my daughter-in-law says she can't WAIT for this book to be finished so she can make all her favourites for her friends and Simon!

Children DO love baking! Recently (when working on a cookbook for beginners) in response to my request, thousands of children wrote to me, telling me all the things they most wanted to cook. Top of the list were cakes!

I hope that you will enjoy the recipes Simon and I have chosen (and simplified where necessary) to suit today's kitchens. Do encourage your children and grandchildren to bake alongside you, so you can introduce them to the joys and satisfactions of cooking. Remember, too, that in passing on these skills, you are perpetuating our country's heritage!

I dedicate this book to my mother, who cooked and baked, with love, for so many people, who taught us so much, by example, and is remembered so fondly by us all.

When you bake, especially if you want good results each time, you need to be precise and measure (or weigh) the ingredients carefully.

The ingredients in these recipes have been measured rather than weighed, and the quantities given in level cup and spoon measures.

We have used standard, metric measuring cups for all the cup measures given. A standard metric measuring cup holds 250 millilitres (quarter of a litre).

A set of "single capacity" measuring cups will enable you to measure all your dry ingredients quickly and easily. Use a set which has a one cup, half cup and quarter cup measure. Occasionally you may see a very small measure which holds an eighth of a cup. This can be useful, but is not essential.

All the dry ingredients you measure in these cups should come right up to the top of the measure, but should not be heaped up in it.

The only ingredient which should be

# Weights and Measures

packed into a cup is brown sugar. Put it in so that it keeps its shape when turned out, like a sand castle.

Flour measurements are especially important when you are baking, since too much will make your mixture stodgy and thick, but too little will make biscuits spread too much, and cause other problems too.

When measuring flour, first stir it lightly in its container, then dip in the measure, lift it out, and level it off with the edge of a knife. Do not shake or bang the measure, since this packs down the flour and means that you will use more than the recipe means you to.

If you prefer to weigh flour, use 130g instead of each cupful listed in the recipe.

Although we used to measure liquids in a clear, graduated measuring cup, we now find it quicker to use the single capacity cups described above, filling them to brimming, each time. (Don't use a wet cup for measuring dry ingredients though,

since some will stick to the cup and your measurements will be inaccurate.)

Larger butter quantities have been given by weight. Butter packs have 50g or 100g markings on them. These are accurate, apart from the markings at each end of the pack. Small quantities of butter have been measured by spoons — one tablespoon of butter weighs nearly 15g. If you don't want to use spoons, cut a 50g slice of butter off the pack and cut it in half for 2 Tbsp, or in quarters for 1 Tbsp.

We have used the original, "plain", paper-wrapped butter in all the recipes where butter is specified. We have not used any softer butters, since we feel that these sometimes produce slightly different results. "Standard" butter contains some salt, so we do not add salt to a recipe with a high proportion of butter. (We DO add salt to recipes using oil or sour cream instead of butter.)

Because household spoons vary so much in size, we always use a set of metric measuring spoons. One tablespoon holds 15ml, and one teaspoon holds 5ml.

All the cup and spoon measures in this

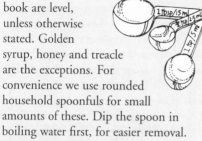

book are level, unless otherwise stated. Golden syrup, honey and treacle are the exceptions. For convenience we use rounded household spoonfuls for small amounts of these. Dip the spoon in boiling water first, for easier removal.

(Remember that a heaped teaspoon holds much more than a level one, and will upset the balance of important ingredients such as baking powder, baking soda and salt in a recipe. Heaped spoons of spices will affect the flavour of the food you are cooking.)

The following abbreviations have been used in this book:

| cm | centimetre | C | Celsius |
|----|------------|------|------------|
| g | gram | ml | millilitre |
| tsp | teaspoon | Tbsp | tablespoon |

The following measures have been used:

| | | |
|---|---|---|
| 1 Tbsp = 3 tsp | | 2 Tbsp = ⅛ cup |
| 4 Tbsp = ¼ cup | | 8 Tbsp = ½ cup |
| 16 Tbsp = 1 cup | | |

# *Before you start mixing...*

There is nothing more annoying than going to the trouble of making something, then being disappointed with the way it turns out. This information should help you produce excellent results when you use our recipes. Please take time to read it before you start mixing, especially if you are an inexperienced baker.

## Cooking times and temperatures

For cakes, biscuits and other baking, your oven must be heated to the right temperature before the food is put in to bake. Turn on the oven before you do anything else!

We positioned our oven racks just below the middle for everything we cooked, since this allowed the top and bottom to brown in about the same time. Ovens vary however, and you may know, or find out quickly, that in your oven, a slightly higher or lower position is better to get this even colouring.

Ovens with fans cook more quickly than ovens without fans set at the same temperature. For this reason, we have often suggested two temperatures. Where we have not, we found that the temperature variation did not matter, as long as we took our baking out when it was done.

If your oven has the option of fan or no fan, you may have already decided which you prefer for baking. If not, we suggest you try baking with the fan. If you don't like your results, next time try the recipe without it. (When we have an option, we bake sponges, cream puffs and rich cakes without a fan, but use it for most other baking.)

We have found that no two ovens cook in exactly the same way! Because of their variations, you must use some judgment, rather than following exact instructions for cooking times. We often offer a range of times, and as well, tell you what to look for, to judge when your baking is ready. Start looking at your food when it has cooked for three quarters of the suggested time, then look every few minutes, until it is at the right stage.

If you like biscuits chewy, don't cook them too long. If you like them really crisp, cook them a little longer.

Cooling on racks produces better results than cooling on the baking tin or tray.

If you have cooked something and found that it was cooked before it browned attractively, turn the oven 5° higher next time.

If it browns before it is cooked in the centre, lower the temperature by the same amount, next time you make it.

Write the exact time and temperature you needed beside the recipe, so you won't have to check it so often next time.

If you feel that your oven is not cooking at the set temperature, buy or borrow an oven thermometer to stand in the middle of your empty, preheated oven. Compare the set temperature with the reading on your thermometer, so you have hard facts to give the service agent!

Celsius Fahrenheit (approx. equivalents)

| | |
|---|---|
| 150°C ... 300°F | 160°C ... 325°F |
| 170°C ... 325°F | 180°C ... 350°F |
| 190°C ... 375°F | 200°C ... 400°F |
| 210°C ... 425°F | 220°C ... 425°F |

# Before you start mixing...

## Stopping food sticking

There are different ways to stop food sticking to oven trays and cake tins. (Always make sure your tins are clean, with a smooth surface.)

Non-stick sprays are very efficient. When using ring tins for delicate cakes, apply an even coating of spray, followed by an even coating of flour. Sieve about ¼ cup of flour into the tin, shake it round to cover all surfaces, then invert the tin and tap to remove excess flour.

Baking paper (baking parchment) works well on biscuit trays, the sides and bottoms of square tins and the bottoms of round and ring tins.

If you bake a lot, consider buying re-usable non-stick Teflon baking pan and tray liners, as we do. Although more expensive, these NEVER stick and are excellent. (Send us a stamped addressed envelope at PO Box 17 016 Wellington for details of prices, weights and shapes.)

Biscuits and cakes baked directly on sprayed surfaces brown more quickly than those on baking paper or Teflon liners. Dark metal tins brown the contents faster than light coloured ones. Glass pans do not brown cakes, etc, well.

## Baking Tins

The baking tins we use most are 23cm round and square tins, and 23cm ring tins (which hold 7 cups of water when filled to the rim). If you don't have a ring tin, use a 20cm round tin of at least the same capacity. We use large and medium-size loaf tins. For our slices, etc, we use sponge roll, lamington, roasting or brownie pans about 20x30cm, or 23cm square tins with removeable bases.

It is not essential to use the exact pan size specified, but remember your results may vary in tins much bigger or smaller. Cakes and slices baked in larger (broader) tins will cook faster and will not rise as high, while those cooked in smaller tins will rise higher (beware of overflows!) and will probably take longer to cook in the middle. Consider using temperatures 5–10° lower if you use smaller tins, too.

## Food Processors

If you have a food processor, you can use it to make some of your baking even quicker and easier, so some of our recipes have food processing instructions as an option.

We use a food processor rather than an electric mixer (except for meringues) but have given emphasis to recipes which can be very simply made without either, and are just stirred together with a spoon, stirrer (see back page) or wire whisk.

## Practical details

Because this book is about practical, everyday family baking, we have simplified and shortened our recipes to suit time restraints and energy levels. This baking is not meant to be "show quality". If you have the time and inclination, however, by all means mix butter and sugar until creamy, and whisk eggs.

If you find that baking left "sitting around" is a temptation, freeze what is not required immediately, bringing it out when you want it. It may often be wrapped and put in lunch boxes while frozen, to thaw as it stands.

# Gingernuts

*These are really easy to make because you stir everything together in a pot.*
*It's fun making lots of little gingernuts instead of big ones!*

**For 80 small biscuits:**
*100g butter*
*1 household Tbsp golden syrup*
*1 cup sugar*
*1–2 tsp ground ginger*
*1 tsp vanilla*
*1 large egg*
*1¾ cups flour*
*1 tsp baking soda*

Turn oven on to 180°C, or to 170°C if using a fan oven (see pages 6 and 7).

Melt the butter in a medium-sized pot or microwave dish. Remove from heat when melted.

Dip an ordinary tablespoon into hot water, then measure the syrup with it. Add the syrup, sugar, ginger (use more for a stronger flavour) and vanilla. Add the egg, then mix well with a stirrer or wooden spoon.

Sift in the flour and baking soda, then mix everything together again.

Stand pot or bowl in cold water to cool the biscuit mixture so it is firmer, then, with wet hands, roll teaspoonfuls of biscuit mixture into small balls. Put these on baking trays lined with baking paper, leaving room to spread.

Bake one tray at a time, for about 10 minutes, until golden brown.

Transfer biscuits on to racks to cool, then store in airtight jars.

# Chocolate Chip Cookies

*These biscuits are enormously popular, and may well become family "staples". They are simple enough for a five-year-old to make, with a little supervision, and if hidden, will keep for weeks in airtight jars!*

**For 24 biscuits:**
*75g butter*
*½ cup brown sugar*
*½ cup white sugar*
*1 large egg*
*½ cup chocolate chips*
*½ tsp baking soda*
*1 cup flour*

Turn the oven on to 180°C.

Microwave the butter in a microwave-proof bowl for 1 minute or melt it in a pot until just liquid. Take off the heat, add both measures of sugar and the egg to the butter and beat with a fork until thoroughly mixed.

Sprinkle the chocolate chips into the bowl. Measure the baking soda and flour into a sieve over the bowl, shake them in, then mix everything together well.

Put a piece of baking paper on an oven tray so the biscuits won't stick. Using two spoons, form half the mixture in 12 piles on the paper, leaving room for spreading.

Bake just below the middle of the oven, for 8–10 minutes or until golden brown, then shape and cook the rest of the mixture in the same way. (A fan oven is likely to cook the biscuits more quickly than a regular oven.)

While biscuits are warm, lift them onto a cooling rack. When cold, store in airtight jars.

# Peanut Brownies

*There may be nothing new or different about peanut brownies, but year after year they remain popular, in lunch boxes, with coffee, and in cafes!*

**For 25–35 biscuits, depending on size:**
*100 g butter*
*½ cup caster or plain sugar*
*1 large egg*
*1 cup flour*
*2 tsp baking powder*
*2 Tbsp cocoa*
*1 cup roasted peanuts (see note below)*

Turn the oven to 180°C, or to 170°C if using a fan oven (see pages 6 and 7).

In a pot or microwave dish, warm the butter until soft but not runny. Whisk (or process) it with the sugar, then add the egg and whisk (or process) again until fluffy.

Using level measuring cups and spoons, measure and sift in the dry ingredients, then stir or process until mixture is smooth. (Peanut brownies should spread a certain amount as they cook — if you use more flour and cocoa than called for, they will not. On the other hand, if they spread too far, not enough flour has been added.) Add the peanuts and stir again.

Using two teaspoons, put spoonfuls of the mixture on a lightly sprayed or buttered oven slide, leaving space for spreading.

Bake for about 15–20 minutes, until the centres feel as firm as the edges.

## Roasted Peanuts

Lightly roasted peanuts have much more flavour than raw ones. Buy good quality, unsalted, or lightly salted roasted peanuts for this recipe.

If salted roasted peanuts seem too salty, rinse them in a sieve, under hot water, then dry them straight away, between paper towels.

To roast raw peanuts, spread on a shallow baking tin and pop them in a hot but turned off oven — by the time the oven and peanuts are cool the peanuts should have changed colour slightly and lost their chewiness.

# Chocolate Crunchies

*This is Alison's simplified version of afghans. Sometimes we ice the biscuits, but they are often left uniced, and disappear almost as quickly!*

**For about 50 biscuits:**
*125g butter*
*1 cup sugar*
*3 Tbsp cocoa*
*1 tsp vanilla*
*1 large egg*
*1 cup self-raising flour*
*1½ cups cornflakes*

**Optional icing and decoration:**
*chocolate icing from page 25 or ½ cup
    chocolate chips and 2 Tbsp sour cream*
*about 50 walnut pieces or halves*

Turn the oven on to 170°C, or to 160°C if using a fan oven (see pages 6 and 7).

In a pot big enough to hold the whole mixture, melt the butter until it is barely liquid, then remove from the heat.

Add the sugar, cocoa, vanilla and egg, and mix well with a fork or stirrer. Measure the flour and slightly crushed cornflakes on top of the mixture and stir until evenly mixed.

Using two teaspoons, put small, compact heaps of the mixture on oven slides which have been lightly buttered, or covered with baking paper. Leave some room for spreading, as these biscuits spread a certain amount as they cook, but if you want large, flatter biscuits you should flatten the unbaked biscuits gently, using several fingers or the pad of your thumb.

Bake for 8–12 minutes until biscuits look evenly cooked and are as firm in the centre as they are near their edges. Transfer to a cooling rack while warm.

If desired, ice and top with walnut halves or pieces before the icing sets.

To make the chocolate chip icing, heat the chocolate chips and sour cream in a microwave or a pot over hot water until you can stir them together to make a smooth mixture. Spread on the biscuits while icing is warm.

Keep iced or uniced biscuits in an airtight container.

# Custard Kisses

*Custard kisses have always been a family favourite! These delicious biscuits are in fact sweet enough to be eaten unfilled, but they taste even better when stuck together with vanilla icing or jam.*

**For about 40 "halves":**
*175g butter*
*1 cup icing sugar*
*1 tsp vanilla*
*1½ cups flour*
*½ cup custard powder*
*1 tsp baking powder*

**Icing:**
*2 Tbsp butter*
*½ cup icing sugar*
*1 Tbsp custard powder*
*a few drops of vanilla essence*

Turn the oven on to 180°C, or to 170°C if using a fan oven (see pages 6 and 7).

Warm butter until very soft but not completely melted. Mix in a large bowl (or process) with the icing sugar and vanilla until creamy, then sift in the flour, custard powder and baking powder. Mix well, squeezing bowl-mixed dough together by hand and adding a little milk if necessary, then shape as below.

Roll mixture into about forty small balls. Flatten each with your hand before putting on an oven tray sprayed with non-stick spray or lined with baking paper, then make a pattern on them with a dampened fork, a meat hammer, the bottom of a patterned glass, or your fingers.

OR, form mixture into a cylinder and refrigerate or freeze until it may be cut without flattening. Cut into about 40 slices, then put on oven tray, decorate as described, or leave plain.

Bake for about 12 minutes, until biscuits feel firm, but have not browned at all. (Browned biscuits taste of burnt butter.)

Cool on a rack, then stick together with icing or raspberry jam.

To make icing, mix softened (but not melted) butter with the other icing ingredients until smooth, adding a few drops of water if necessary. (For a generous filling, double the recipe.)

Store in airtight containers when icing has set. Freeze for longer storage.

**VARIATION:** For Almond Creams, add ¼ tsp almond essence and ¼ cup of lightly toasted flaked almonds to the biscuit mixture, and a few drops of almond essence to the filling. Replace custard powder with cornflour if you like.

# Peanut Plus Cookies

*Whatever age you are, we think that you'll enjoy a glass of milk and one of these peanutty cookies, full of good things! Make them giant-sized for fun, or regular size if you want them to last longer.*

**24 10cm, or up to 60 smaller biscuits:**
*50g butter*
*¼ cup golden syrup*
*¾ cup peanut butter (crunchy or plain)*
*1 large egg*
*1 tsp vanilla*
*½ cup white sugar*
*½ cup brown sugar*
*½ cup each sultanas, roasted salted
    peanuts, chocolate chips*
*½ cup sunflower seeds, optional*
*1¾ cups flour*
*1 tsp baking soda*

Turn the oven on to 180°C, or to 170°C if using a fan oven (see pages 6 and 7).

In a large pot or microwave bowl melt the butter and the golden syrup (measured with a hot wet measuring cup) just until you can stir them together without any lumps of butter showing. Stop heating, then stir in the peanut butter until mixture is smooth.

Add the egg, vanilla and sugars and beat with a fork or stirrer until evenly mixed, then add the sultanas, roughly chopped peanuts, chocolate chips and sunflower seeds, if using.

Measure the flour and soda into a sieve over the bowl or pot, shake it in, and mix until evenly combined.

With wet hands divide the mixture into balls. For giant biscuits make 24 balls. Place 6 at a time on a baking tray lined with baking paper, then flatten with wet

fingers until biscuits measure 9cm across.

**NOTE:** (Biscuits spread 1cm during cooking.) For smaller biscuits, make 36–60 balls, then flatten until they are about 7mm thick.

Bake for 7–10 minutes, until evenly golden brown. Take from oven before biscuits brown around the edge. (Use a slightly shorter time for chewy biscuits.) Cool on a rack and store in sealed plastic bags or in other airtight containers.

**NOTE:** To cook giant biscuits more evenly, reduce heat by 10°C and cook 2–3 minutes longer, if preferred.

# Easy Oaty Cookies

*Alison is a strong believer in the goodness of rolled oats! Although she can not always persuade her family to eat porridge, there is no problem with these biscuits which are extra-good packed for play-lunch or for after-school snacks.*

**For about 60 biscuits, depending on size:**
*200g butter*
*1 cup soft brown sugar*
*1 cup white sugar*
*1 large egg*
*¼ cup milk*
*½ tsp baking soda*
*1 tsp vanilla*
*1 cup flour*
*3 cups rolled oats (not whole-grain oats)*
*½ cup sultanas, optional*
*½ cup chopped walnuts, optional*
*½ cup sunflower seeds, optional*

Turn oven to 180°C, or to 170°C if using a fan oven (see pages 6 and 7).

Melt the butter in a large pot or microwaveable bowl, removing from the heat as soon as it is liquid.

Stir in the sugars and egg, then the milk, soda and vanilla stirred together.

Sprinkle the flour, rolled oats and optional additions over everything else and mix well with a stirrer, spoon or fork until well combined.

Drop mixture in teaspoon lots on an oven slide sprayed with non-stick spray or covered with baking paper, leaving room for spreading.

Bake for 10–12 minutes, or until biscuits are golden brown and feel firm. Shape another trayful of biscuits while the one before it cooks.

Lift onto wire rack while warm. (Biscuits which have cooled too much are hard to lift off, so put the tray back in the oven for about a minute if this happens.) When cold, store in airtight containers.

*Photograph shown on page 14*

# Almond Crisps

*Flecked with toasted almonds, these buttery, crisp biscuits are irresistible!*

**For about 30 biscuits:**
*¼–½ cup toasted slivered almonds*
*100g soft butter*
*½ cup sugar*
*about ½ tsp almond essence*
*½ cup flour*
*½ cup self-raising flour*

Turn the oven on to 170°C, or to 160°C if using a fan oven (see pages 6 and 7). While it heats, toast the slivered (or chopped) almonds which you have spread on a shallow baking dish. Watch them carefully, removing them as soon as they have browned lightly.

Soften but do not melt the butter. Mix the butter, sugar and essence in a food processor, then add everything else without sifting, and process briefly to mix.

OR beat in the sugar and essence using a stirrer or wooden spoon. Stir together the flours or shake them through a sieve into the bowl. Add the almonds and stir everything together until well mixed.

Form dough into a cylinder on a floured board and chill in the refrigerator or freezer until it is firm enough to cut into thin slices.

Bake on an oven slide (which has been lightly buttered, sprayed or lined with baking paper) for about 10 minutes or until edges colour slightly. Cool slightly, then lift onto a cooling rack.

When cold, store in an airtight container.

**NOTE:** If butter is too liquid and mixture too crumbly to handle, add a little milk until dough sticks together.

**VARIATIONS:** For Almond and Cherry Crisps, add 6 finely chopped, crystallised cherries to the mixture.

For almond or cherry topped biscuits, leave out the toasted almonds, roll into balls, flatten slightly, then top with whole almonds or halved cherries. For Walnut Crisps, replace almonds with ½ cup chopped (untoasted) walnuts.

# Spicy Dutch Biscuits

*Rolling and cutting this (well refrigerated) mixture is something of a family tradition in our house.*
*Even little hands can help, and the resulting biscuits make most acceptable gifts.*

**For about 100 biscuits:**

*3 cups flour*
*2 tsp baking powder*
*2 tsp cinnamon*
*½ tsp of each: ground cloves, coriander,*
*    nutmeg and cardamom*
*225g butter, softened*
*1 ¼ cups brown sugar*
*¼ cup milk*

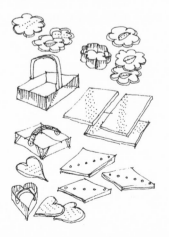

Turn the oven to 180°C, or to 170°C if using a fan oven (see pages 6 and 7).

Sift the flour, baking powder and spices through a sieve into a large bowl.

Rub the softened, but not completely melted, butter through the dry ingredients, then add the sugar and milk. Mix, first with a stirrer, then with your hands until mixture forms a ball, then transfer to a plastic bag and refrigerate until cool and firm.

Roll out about a quarter of the dough at a time (keeping the remaining dough cool) on a well floured surface, and cut into shapes with cutters.

To make this easier for little helpers, use plenty of dusting flour and dip the cutters into extra flour before using them. Lifting the cut shapes carefully using a fish slice helps prevent distortion.

Bake for about 8–15 minutes or until lightly browned, remembering that cooking time depends on biscuit thickness. Cool on a rack, then store in an airtight container.

The full flavour does not develop until a few hours after baking. These crisp little biscuits are good just as they are and do not need decorating.

**VARIATION:** Roll the dough into two long cylinders. Chill, then cut each cylinder into about 50 thin slices. Lay these on the baking sheet covered with baking paper, prick each in a few places, and bake as for the cut-out biscuits. Cool on a rack. Store in an airtight jar when cool.

**NOTE:** For well flavoured biscuits, make sure the spices are fresh and aromatic.

# Belgian Biscuits

*This spicy mixture is very popular made into biscuits, but is equally delicious and even simpler when made into a square!*

**For 75 biscuits or about 20 squares:**
*1 cup brown sugar, packed*
*200g butter, softened*
*1 large egg*
*1 tsp cinnamon*
*2 tsp mixed spice*
*4 tsp baking powder*
*2 cups flour*
*about ¼ cup raspberry jam*

**Icing:**
*2 cups icing sugar*
*25g butter, softened*
*lemon juice or water*

**Decoration:**
*raspberry jelly crystals, optional*

Measure the brown sugar, softened butter and egg into a food processor or large bowl. Mix well, then add all the dry ingredients except the flour. Mix or process again, then add and mix in half the flour. Add remaining flour and process in short bursts until mixed, or stir with a spatula until well mixed.

For a square, divide the dough into two halves, refrigerate until firm enough to roll. Roll each half into a 20x25cm rectangle. (Work the dough between sheets of waxed paper or plastic to prevent sticking.)

Place the first sheet on a non-stick sprayed and/or baking paper lined baking sheet, then spread with thin layer of jam. Cover with the second sheet of dough and bake at 160°C for 20–30 minutes until the centre is firm when gently pressed. Cool, ice if desired and cut into squares.

For biscuits, gently form dough into three sausage-shaped rolls, each about 5cm in diameter. Refrigerate until firm, then cut each roll into about 25 thin slices.

Place biscuits on a non-stick sprayed oven slide, leaving space for spreading. Bake at 170°C for about 10 minutes, or until the edges show signs of darkening. Cool on racks while the next batch cooks.

Store in an airtight container 'as is', or sandwich together with raspberry jam.

If desired, top with icing. Beat icing sugar and butter with enough lemon juice or water (about 3 Tbsp) to make a fairly soft icing. Before icing sets, sprinkle with red jelly crystals if desired.

# Oaty Fingers

*These can be mixed in seconds, rolled out directly on the baking sheet, then baked – they couldn't be any easier!*
*Delicious served plain or buttered, whichever you prefer.*

**For about 20 fingers:**
*100g soft butter*
*½ cup brown sugar*
*½ cup flour*
*½ cup fine rolled oats*
*½ cup oat bran*
*¼ cup toasted sesame seeds, optional*

Turn oven to 180°C, or to 170°C if using a fan oven (see pages 6 and 7).

Soften but do not melt the butter. Mix well with the sugar, then with the remaining ingredients by hand or better still in food processor bowl, adding 1–2 tablespoons of water if dough will not stick together.

Transfer dough to a baking paper covered oven tray (or roll on bench) and roll out, under a sheet of plastic, to a 5mm thickness. Mark dough into rectangles about 25x100mm but don't separate the biscuits until baked.

Bake for 10–15 minutes, until golden brown. Leave to cool on the tray, then separate into individual fingers.

Enjoy immediately or store in an airtight container

# Pikelets

*Pikelets are great for a quick snack or for unexpected company. Spread them with butter and jam, top them with hundreds and thousands for small children, or 'dress them up' with whipped cream, jam and fresh berries for a treat!*

**For 12–20 pikelets:**

1 household Tbsp golden syrup
25g butter
1 Tbsp sugar
½ cup milk*
1 large egg
1 cup self-raising flour

\* *For very tender pikelets replace ½ cup milk with ¾ cup buttermilk.*

Heat a frypan. (Use a high heat setting if frypan is electric.)

Dip a household tablespoon in hot water, then use it to measure the syrup. Put the syrup into a bowl with butter. Warm to soften both, then mix in the sugar, milk and egg.

Sprinkle the flour over the top, then mix briefly with a whisk or beater just until smooth.

Rub surface of the hot frypan with a little butter on a paper towel. Drop tablespoonfuls of mixture into the pan, pouring mixture off the tip of the spoon to make nice round pikelets.

As soon as the bubbles begin to burst on the surface, turn pikelets over. (Turn up the heat if the pikelets are not brown enough OR turn heat down if they are too brown when the first bubbles burst.)

When the centres of the second side spring back when touched with your finger, the pikelets are ready.

(If pikelets are too thick and are not spreading enough, add a little extra milk to mixture.)

Cook in batches until all the batter is used. Keep soft by putting hot pikelets between the folds of a clean teatowel, and transfer to a plastic bag when cold.

Serve warm, as described above.

# Lemonade & Cream Scones

*No baking book would be complete without a scone recipe! We find this untraditional version so easy, good and reliable, we will probably never go back to grandma's version! We think that you will probably agree.*

**For 8 large square scones:**
*2 cups (260g) self-raising flour*
*¼ cup sugar*
*½ tsp salt*
*½ cup cream*
*½ cup plus 2 Tbsp lemonade*

Turn oven on to 230°C, or to 220°C if using a fan oven (see pages 6 and 7).

Measure the dry ingredients into a large bowl. (Remember to fork the flour until light before measuring it, then to spoon it into the measuring cup and level off the top without packing it down or banging it.) Toss dry ingredients together, add the cream and lemonade, and mix to make a soft dough.

Scrape the sides of the bowl and sprinkle enough extra flour over the ball of soft dough to allow you to turn it out onto a floured board and handle it without sticking.

Knead dough lightly, half a dozen times, then pat or roll it out until it is about 2cm thick, and twice as long as it is wide.

Cut in half lengthwise, and in four crosswise, using a floured knife.

Arrange scones on a baking tray (close together if you like soft sides, or further apart for crusty sides). For a good colour, brush tops with a little milk or melted butter if you like.

Bake for 10–12 minutes, until tops and bottoms are lightly browned.

Serve warm (or reheated), split, with butter and jam, or spread with jam and topped with whipped cream. If available, fresh strawberries or raspberries make an excellent addition.

NOTE: These scones stay fresh and soft for 48 hours — if they get the chance!

# Chocolate Fudge Square

*This delicious (unbaked) fudge square is simple enough to be made by quite inexperienced young cooks - show them how to do it once or twice, then they can easily make it on their own!*

**For 12–24 slices, depending on size:**
250g packet Malt, Wine or Digestive
    biscuits, crushed
½ cup brown sugar
¼ cup cocoa
3 Tbsp milk
75g butter
about 1 cup chopped walnuts or chopped
    sultanas, or a mixture of both
1 tsp vanilla

**Chocolate Icing:**
1 Tbsp cocoa
2 Tbsp boiling water
1 Tbsp butter
½ tsp vanilla
1 cup icing sugar

To crush the biscuits, put them in a large plastic bag, fasten loosely with a rubber band, then bang and roll with a rolling pin until quite evenly crushed. (Crumb broken biscuits in a food processor if you like, but don't make evenly fine crumbs.)

Mix the sugar and cocoa in a medium-sized pot or pan, then stir in the milk, and add the butter. Bring to the boil, stirring all the time.

Remove from the heat, add the crushed biscuits, chopped nuts and/or sultanas and the essence, and stir together.

Press mixture into a baking paper lined 20x30cm sponge roll tin (you do not have to spread the mixture over the whole tin) until it is the depth you like. Flatten surface fairly smoothly with the back of a spoon.

Ice with chocolate icing (or sour cream icing, page 11). Measure the cocoa into a small bowl, add the boiling water and mix to a paste. Add the butter, vanilla and (sifted) icing sugar and beat until smooth. (Adjust thickness by adding a little extra water or icing sugar if necessary).

Cut into pieces when firm. Store in the refrigerator in hot weather.

**VARIATIONS:** Add peppermint essence to both the base and icing.

Use finely grated tangelo or orange rind in the base and/or the icing for a jaffa flavour.

Add rum essence to the base and icing instead of, or as well as, the vanilla.

# Orange Slice

*Kirsten learned how to make this, her favourite slice, when she was eight years old! It is now a popular addition to her children's lunch boxes. Replace the orange with other citrus fruit if you like — all are good.*

**For about 24 slices:**
*100g butter*
*½ a 400g can sweetened condensed milk*
*finely grated rind of 1 orange*
*1 cup fine desiccated coconut*
*1 packet (225g) wine biscuits*

**Orange Icing:**
*25g (2 Tbsp) butter*
*1 cup icing sugar*
*about 1 Tbsp orange juice*

Warm the first amount of butter in a medium sized pot or microwave dish until melted. Remove from the heat and stir in the condensed milk.

Finely grate all the coloured rind from an orange. Add the rind and coconut to the butter mixture, then stir until well combined.

Break the biscuits into halves or quarters. Put the pieces in a big plastic bag, close bag loosely, and bang the bag with a rolling pin until all the biscuits are crumbed, then stir them into the pot. (If you like, crumb the biscuits in a food processor, then add the other ingredients and mix well.)

Press mixture into a buttered tin about 23 cm square. (For a thicker slice, use a smaller tin or press mixture into only part of a bigger tin.) Push mixture down firmly and level the top.

To make the icing, put the second measure of butter in a clean bowl. It should be soft enough to mix easily, but not melted. Add the icing sugar and enough juice to mix with a stirrer, or table knife so it will spread smoothly over the base.

Pattern the icing by making wiggles on top with a fork, then chill until firm.

Cut into fingers, rectangles or squares.

Keep in a covered container in a fridge, up to a week, or in a freezer for up to 3 months.

**VARIATION:** Replace orange rind and juice with lemon rind and juice.

# Super Muesli Bars

*Muesli bars are really quite easy to make, and home-made bars cost a fraction of the price of bought bars. Toasting the grains first does add an additional step, but gives the bars a delicious nutty flavour.*

**For about 12-20 bars:**
*1 cup rolled oats*
*½ cup wheatgerm*
*½ cup sesame seeds*
*½ cup sunflower seeds*
*¼ cup dried apricots, chopped, optional*
*50g butter or ¼ cup oil*
*½ cup honey*
*¼ cup peanut butter*

Mix the first four ingredients together in a sponge roll tin or heavy frying pan.

Lightly toast the mixture, by cooking about 10cm below a grill or on the stove-top over a medium heat, until it has coloured lightly and lost its raw taste. (This should take 5–6 minutes.) Stir frequently to ensure nothing burns.

Briefly run the dried apricots under the hot tap, then chop them finely and set aside.

While the oat mixture is browning, measure the butter or oil, honey and peanut butter into a large frypan. Bring to the boil over moderate heat, stirring to blend the ingredients, then turn the heat very low and cook the mixture gently until it forms a firm ball when a little is dropped into cold water and left for about 1 minute.

Stir the lightly browned oat mixture and chopped apricots into the syrup until evenly mixed. Carefully press the hot mixture into a lightly buttered or oiled 20cm square, loose-bottomed tin using the back of a spoon.

Leave the mixture to cool until firm but still flexible, then turn it out and cut into fingers or bars of the desired size. (A sharp serrated knife seems to work best for this.)

Wrap bars individually in cling wrap, or store in a completely airtight container. (Like toffee, they soften and turn sticky if left uncovered.)

# Coconut Whiskers

*These delicious (and flourless) biscuits are unbelievably quick and really couldn't be much simpler.*
*This is another great recipe to teach your kids!*

**For about 20 whiskers:**
*50g butter*
*½ cup sugar*
*½ tsp vanilla*
*1 large egg*
*1 ¼ – 1 ¾ cups desiccated coconut\**

*\* Use 1 ¼ cups fine coconut*
  *Use 1 ½ cups medium coconut*
  *Use 1 ¾ cups thread coconut*

Turn oven to 180°C, or to 170°C if using a fan oven (see pages 6 and 7).

Melt the butter in a pot or microwave dish. Take off the heat, add the remaining ingredients in the order given, and stir with a fork until evenly mixed.

Use two teaspoons for shaping — take a spoonful of the mixture and push it on a non-stick sprayed or baking paper covered oven slide with the other spoon. The biscuits will be almost the same size and shape after baking, so leave them shaped like haystacks or flatten them with your fingers or with the back of a wet spoon, depending on the shape you want.

Bake for 12–15 minutes until the bottom edges and the "whiskery" bits are golden. Watch closely towards the end of the cooking time, since biscuits should not brown too much, and the centres should be moist and slightly chewy.

Lift from the baking tray to a cooling rack straight away, leave to cool, then store in an airtight container.

# Nana's Cheesecake Tarts

*My mother (Nana to my children) always had a tin of these little tarts — they have now been enjoyed by four generations of our family. I was quite overwhelmed when my daughter brought me a batch of them, several years after my mother's death.*

**For 24 tarts:**

*Pastry\*:*
1 cup (130g) flour
75g cold butter
3–4 Tbsp water

*Filling:*
125 g butter, cubed
½ cup sugar
2 large eggs
1 cup (130g) flour
1 tsp baking powder
1 tsp vanilla
¼ cup raspberry jam

*\*Make your own pastry or use very thinly rolled bought flaky pastry instead.*

Turn oven to 190°C, or to 180°C if using a fan oven (see pages 6 and 7).

If using home-made pastry, make it first. Measure the flour and cold, cubed butter into a food processor. Process briefly while adding just enough water, a few drops at a time, to make the particles stick together. Remove from the food processor, form into a ball and chill, while you mix the cake mixture.

Whisk or process the softened but not melted butter and sugar together until creamy. Add one egg and half the flour, mix until just combined, then add remaining egg, flour, baking powder and vanilla, and mix briefly again.

Roll out the bought or homemade pastry thinly, and cut circles to fit 18–24 small patty pans. Place about half a teaspoon of jam on each pastry circle, then add a spoonful of the cake mixture.

If you like, roll out the scraps of pastry, cut into 5mm strips, and place a strip on top of each uncooked cake.

Bake for about 15 minutes, until lightly browned, and until the centre of each little cake springs back when pressed.

Remove from tins, cool on a cake rack, then store in an airtight container. These are nicest eaten within a day or two of baking.

# Rock Cakes

*When I asked my husband which of his mother's recipes he remembered most fondly, he answered "Rock Cakes!". An uninspiring name perhaps, but these easy little cakes disappear fast enough to show that old fashioned baking is still very popular.*

**For 30–40 rock cakes:**

*125 g butter*
*½ cup sugar*
*½ tsp vanilla*
*1 egg*
*¾ cup (95g) self-raising flour*
*1 cup (130g) plain flour*
*1 cup currants, sultanas, or mixed fruit*

Turn the oven on to 180°C, or to 170°C if using a fan oven (see pages 6 and 7).

Soften but do not melt the butter. Add the sugar and vanilla, whisk or food process to combine, then add the egg and a tablespoon of the measured flour, and whisk or food process until light coloured. Add the remaining flours, and mix just enough to combine. Add the dried fruit and stir or process very briefly.

Using two spoons, form into mounds on a non-stick sprayed or baking paper-lined oven tray, leaving a little space for spreading.

Bake for 10–15 minutes, until golden at the edges, and firm in the middle.

Cool on a rack, then store in an airtight container.

NOTE: For best results, sift flour with a fork before spooning it into the cup measures. Do not pack it into the cups (see page 4). Rock cakes which spread a lot do not have quite enough flour, and those which stay exactly as shaped and do not flatten at all contain too much flour.

# Almond Rosettes

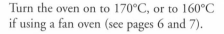

*These biscuits are really quick and easy to make using a food processor. Piping the mixture makes them extra special — if you don't have a forcing bag, shape the biscuits by pushing them through a heavy-weight plastic bag with the corner cut out.*

### For 24–36 rosettes:

*2 large egg whites*
*¼ cup caster sugar*
*1 ¼ cups (125g) ground almonds*
*¼ tsp salt*
*about ¼ tsp almond essence*
*8–16 glace cherries*

Turn the oven on to 170°C, or to 160°C if using a fan oven (see pages 6 and 7).

Put the first four ingredients into a food processor. Mix until well blended and fairly smooth. If the mixture looks too soft to keep its shape at the end of this time, add more ground almonds.

Add almond essence to taste. The biscuits should taste definitely, but not too strongly, of almonds. Mix again.

Cover an oven tray with baking paper and coat with non-stick spray as a precaution, since these biscuits have a definite tendency to stick.

Pipe or otherwise shape the mixture into rosettes, making 24–36 biscuits. As the biscuits do not spread during cooking, you can put them quite close together.

Cut the cherries into halves or quarters, and press them into the uncooked biscuit dough.

Bake for about 15 minutes, until the biscuits are golden brown all over. If they appear to be browning too soon, turn the oven down 10°C.

Cool on a rack, then store in air-tight jars.

NOTE: To make these without a food processor, whisk or beat the egg whites until bubbly but not stiff, add the remaining ingredients, and whisk/beat well until the mixture becomes quite stiff.

# Economical Meringues

*Whenever I have an egg white left over, I put it aside for these meringues — try them if you have an electric beater.*
*If cooked until they are completely dry, the meringues can be stored (well hidden!) in an airtight container for several months.*

**For 50–60 meringues:**
*1 large egg white*
*¾ cup sugar*
*1 tsp vinegar*
*1 tsp vanilla*
*2 Tbsp boiling water*

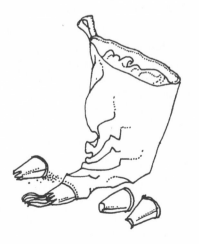

Turn the oven to 150°C, or to 140°C if using a fan oven (see pages 6 and 7).

Measure all the ingredients, in the order given, into the small bowl of an electric beater. (The mixture will look watery and unlikely but it does work!) Stand the bowl inside a larger container that is filled with very hot water.

Using highest speed, beat until the mixture is smooth, stiff and piled high.

Cover a large oven tray with baking paper (using a few small dabs of mixture to stick it down and prevent curling up). Using a forcer bag with a star nozzle, a thick plastic bag with the corner cut out, or two teaspoons, shape the mixture into 50–60 small meringues.

Bake for an hour or until dried through. If you are not sure whether they are cooked, lift one off the paper, and let it cool. When cooked, it will be dry right through, when you break it.

As soon as the meringues are cold, store them in airtight containers.

NOTE: I have never made these using a hand beater. I suppose it can be done, but only if you have a strong arm and a large degree of patience.

# Sticky Gingerbread

*This type of gingerbread reminds Alison of welcome tearoom stops in Yorkshire, after walking for hours through beautiful countryside.*

**For a 20cm square gingerbread:**
*125g butter*
*¾ cup (packed) brown sugar*
*¾ cup golden syrup*
*1 Tbsp grated root ginger, if available*
*1 large egg*
*½ cup plus 2 Tbsp milk*
*2 cups flour*
*2 (or 3) tsp ground ginger*
*1 tsp baking soda*

Turn oven to 160°C, or to 150°C if using a fan oven (see pages 6 and 7).

Stand the tin of golden syrup in a bowl of hot water and line the bottom and sides of a 20cm square baking pan with two strips of baking paper.

Warm the butter in a pot or large microwave-proof dish until it has just melted, then add the brown sugar (firmly pressed into the measure/s). Rinse a measuring cup with hot water and pour the softened syrup into it. Add this to the butter with the grated root ginger (if using) and the egg, then beat with a whisk (or fork) to combine thoroughly.

Without mixing it in, add the milk, then stand a sieve over the pot or bowl and measure into it the flour, the ground ginger (using the larger amount if you didn't add the root ginger) and baking soda. Shake these into the bowl then stir everything together until smooth and somewhat thinner than a usual cake mixture.

OR measure everything, in the order given (without sifting the dry ingredients) into a food processor. Process in short bursts, for about 30 seconds or until evenly mixed.

Pour into the paper-lined pan and bake for about an hour or until the centre springs back when pressed gently with a finger, and a skewer inserted in the middle comes out clean.

Cool in the baking pan on a cooling rack, and store in a loosely covered container.

Eat warm, reheated or cold, buttered.

# Chocolate Cake

*My daughter Kirsten has made this cake for years with great success. It is enormously popular at birthday parties or as a weekend treat!*

**For a 23cm round cake:**
125g butter
½ cup golden syrup
2 large eggs
1½ cups milk
1 cup sugar
2 cups plain flour
¼ cup cocoa
2 tsp baking powder
2 tsp baking soda

**Chocolate Icing:**
2 Tbsp butter
1 Tbsp cocoa
2 Tbsp water
1½ cups icing sugar

*Whipped cream, if you like*

Turn oven to 180°C, or to 170°C if using a fan oven (see pages 6 and 7).

Line the bottom of a 23cm round cake tin (see note) with baking paper and non-stick spray its sides.

Melt the butter in a pot, then remove from the heat. Dip a measuring cup in hot water and use this to measure in the syrup. Mix butter and syrup together.

Put eggs, milk and sugar in a food processor or large bowl. Process or whisk until well mixed.

Measure the flour, cocoa, baking powder and soda into sieve over the bowl, and shake in. Process in very short bursts, or stir until just mixed, then add the melted butter and syrup. Mix or process briefly again. (Do not overmix!) Pour mixture into the prepared tin.

Bake for 40 minutes or until the centre feels firm and a skewer poked into the middle comes out clean.

Cool cake on rack. If you like, cut cake in half and fill with whipped cream.

Dust with icing sugar, or make icing. Warm the butter, cocoa and water together until butter melts. Take off the heat, sift in icing sugar and mix until smooth. Spread on the cake.

**NOTE:** If you prefer, bake this cake in a 23x33cm tin or two 20cm round tins.

# Easy Banana Cake

*This popular cake provides the perfect way to use up brown-flecked bananas which have ripened while your back was turned, or which are on sale cheaply, because they are too ripe to eat in hand!*

**For a 23cm ring cake or a large loaf:**
*150g butter, melted*
*1–1¼ cups ripe, mashed banana*
    *(3 bananas)*
*½ cup white sugar*
*½ cup brown sugar*
*1 tsp vanilla*
*2 large eggs*
*½ cup milk*
*2 cups self-raising flour*

Turn oven to 180°C, or to 170°C if using a fan oven (see pages 6 and 7).

Melt the butter until liquid in a large bowl in a microwave oven, or in a large pot, preferably with rounded corners, then remove from heat.

Mash the bananas with a fork, working from one end to the other, without leaving chunks. (Slightly overripe bananas give the cake best flavour.)

Spoon mashed banana into measuring cup to get an idea of the amount used, then tip into the pot with the sugars, vanilla and eggs.

Beat with a fork, stirrer or whisk until the eggs are well blended, then stir in the milk, mix in, then add the flour.

Beat with the whisk or stirrer until evenly mixed, then pour into a 23cm (7 cup capacity) ring pan or large loaf tin of the same capacity, which has been well coated with non-stick spray.

Bake for 40–50 minutes, until top is golden brown, the centre springs back when pressed, and a skewer poked into the middle comes out clean. (Don't worry if the top cracks slightly.) Leave stand in the tin for 5 minutes, then invert onto a cooling rack.

Serve plain or dusted with icing sugar, preferably within a few hours of baking.

Particularly nice served warm, as above or with icecream and fresh fruit, for dessert.

# Elizabeth's Carrot Cake

*Alison's granddaughter, aged 12, liked this cake enough to make it by herself! It is always very popular and is certainly a great way to eat carrots! (Use a food processor for grating and mixing if you have one.)*

### For a 20cm round or square cake:
2 cups finely grated carrot
2 large eggs
1 cup brown sugar
¾ cup canola (or other) oil
1 tsp vanilla
1 tsp grated lemon or orange rind
1¼ cups plain flour
2 tsp cinnamon
2 tsp mixed spice
1 tsp baking soda
1 tsp salt

### Lemon icing:
1 Tbsp butter, warmed
½ tsp finely grated lemon rind
1½ Tbsp lemon juice
about 1½ cups icing sugar

Turn the oven on to 180°C, or to 170°C if using a fan oven (see pages 6 and 7).

Line the sides and bottom of a 20cm square cake tin with two strips of baking paper. (Each strip should cover 2 sides and the bottom.)

Grate the carrots finely in a food processor or hand grater, measuring them by pressing them into the cup. Put aside.

Process or beat the eggs, sugar, oil, vanilla and rind together until thick and smooth. Add the grated carrot and mix in thoroughly.

Measure the flour, cinnamon, mixed spice, baking soda and salt into a sieve over the bowl and shake in. Process briefly or fold together, without overmixing, then pour into the lined tin.

Bake for 45 minutes or until centre is firm and a skewer comes out clean. (The cake may rise up in the middle, but it is still fine!)

Cool in the tin for 15 minutes, then carefully transfer to a rack.

To make the icing, warm the butter until soft. Add the finely grated lemon rind and lemon juice, then stir in enough sifted icing sugar to make icing which is not runny. Spread carefully over the cake.

Cut the cake when icing is cold.

36

# Crazy Cake

*This may seem an odd name for a cake, but there are not too many recipes that work so well without eggs, butter, milk or an egg beater. Its surprisingly good texture and interesting flavour make it well worth trying!*

**For a 23cm ring or 20cm square cake:**
*1½ cups flour*
*2 Tbsp cocoa*
*1 tsp each cinnamon and ginger*
*1 tsp baking soda*
*1 tsp salt*
*1 cup sugar*
*½ cup canola or other oil*
*¾ cup water*
*2 Tbsp vinegar*
*1 tsp vanilla*

Turn the oven to 190°C, or to 180°C if using a fan oven (see pages 6 and 7).

Before you start mixing, line the bottom of a 23cm ring tin, or the bottom and two sides of a 20cm square tin with baking paper. Butter, or non-stick spray, then flour the uncovered sides of the tin.

Measure the first six ingredients into a sieve, and sift them into a fairly large bowl. Add the sugar and stir well with a fork. Measure the oil and add it to the dry ingredients, without stirring.

Measure the water, vinegar and vanilla together, then add these to the flour-oil mixture. Stir with the fork until the mixture is smooth and no dry lumps remain.

Pour the mixture into the prepared tin and bake for 30–40 minutes, until the centre of the cake springs back when touched with the finger, and a toothpick or skewer comes out clean.

Leave cake in the tin for 4–5 minutes, then turn out onto a wire rack and leave to cool. Dust with sieved icing sugar.

Serve cut in fairly thick slices, or, serve squares of cake for dessert, topped with whipped cream and raspberry or blackcurrant jam.

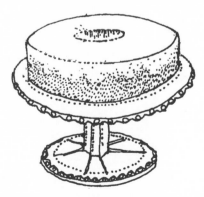

# Lemon (or Orange) Cream Cake

*This cake is a cross between a sponge cake and a buttercake. Cream replaces butter, so there is no need to bother with softening or creaming, and the ingredients are easy to combine.*

**For a 23cm ring cake or 20cm round cake:**

*2 large eggs*
*1 cup sugar*
*1 cup cream*
*finely grated rind of 2 lemons or 1 large orange*
*1 cup (130g) plain flour*
*1 cup (130g) self-raising flour*
*2 Tbsp lemon or orange juice*

Turn the oven to 180°C, or to 170°C if using a fan oven (see pages 6 and 7).

Spray a 23cm ring pan thoroughly with non-stick spray, then dust liberally with flour, banging tin to remove excess.

Put the eggs, sugar and cream in a medium-sized bowl and beat until the sugar has dissolved and the mixture has thickened slightly. Grate onto it all the coloured rind from the lemons or orange, then stir in the sifted flours and the juice until the mixture is thick and smooth. (Make sure that you do not add extra flour to this cake. Stir the flour with a fork to aerate and lighten it before measuring it, then spoon it lightly into the measuring cups without banging cups or compacting the flour.)

Coat a 23cm ring tin or 20cm round tin with non-stick spray, then dust with flour. Tap inverted tin to dislodge extra flour. Pour the mixture into the prepared tin.

Bake for 25–40 minutes or until the centre springs back when pressed with a finger and a skewer comes out clean.

Dust cake with icing sugar or ice it with lemon or orange icing (using the recipe on page 26).

Eat the cake within two or three days.

# Kirsten's Chocolate Roll

*For years Kirsten asked for this cake for every birthday party she had. It is quickly made, always looks good and tastes delicious! Remember to use level, standard measures when measuring the cocoa.*

### For one sponge roll:
3 large eggs
½ cup sugar
½ cup flour
2 Tbsp cocoa
1 tsp baking powder
1 Tbsp boiling water

### Filling:
¼–½ cup raspberry jam
1–1½ cups cream, whipped

Turn the oven to 230°C, or to 220°C if using a fan oven (see pages 6 and 7).

Beat eggs and sugar together until mixture is very thick and creamy. (For best results use room temperature eggs rather than those straight from the fridge.)

Measure flour, cocoa and baking powder into a sieve over the egg mixture, and gently shake them through. Carefully fold them into the egg mixture, then add the boiling water and mix again. Spread mixture evenly into a medium to large sponge roll tin lined with baking paper.

Bake for 8–10 minutes, or until the centre of the sponge springs back when pressed lightly with a finger. (Take care not to overcook.) Working quickly, loosen the sponge from the sides of the tin, and turn it out on to a clean piece of fine cotton (muslin or soft, old tea towel) that has been wetted, then wrung out as dry as possible. Lift the baking paper off the sponge, and roll sponge and tea towel together, lightly but firmly. (Roll either way, depending whether you want a short thick or a long thin roll.)

Stand roll, still in towel, on a rack until cold, then unroll carefully. Spread with raspberry jam and whipped cream and roll up again (without the teatowel!).

Sprinkle with icing sugar just before serving. (This cake is best eaten the day it is made, although slightly soft leftovers taste good the next day.)

# Lemon Yoghurt Cake

*Because this cake contains oil rather than butter, it is very easy to mix, either in a food processor, or in a bowl using a whisk or fork.*

**For a 23cm ring cake:**

1¾ cups sugar
rind of 2 lemons
2 large eggs
1 cup canola or other oil
½ tsp salt
1 cup yoghurt
2–3 Tbsp lemon juice
2 cups self-raising flour

Turn oven on to 190°C, or to 180°C if using a fan oven (see pages 6 and 7).

If you are using a food processor, put the sugar into the (dry) bowl with the metal chopping blade. Peel all the yellow peel from the lemons, using a potato peeler, and add to the bowl. Run the machine until the lemon peel is finely chopped through the sugar.

Add the eggs, oil and salt and process until thick and smooth, then add the yoghurt and lemon juice and blend enough to mix. (Use plain, sweetened or flavoured yoghurt. If you use flavoured yoghurt, choose a flavour that will blend with the colour and flavour of the lemon.) Add the flour and process just enough to combine with the rest of the mixture.

To mix by hand, grate all the coloured peel from the lemons into a large bowl.

Add the sugar, eggs and oil, then whisk together. Add the salt, yoghurt and lemon juice and mix again. Sift in the flour, then mix gently until just combined.

Pour cake mixture into a non-stick, sprayed and floured 23cm ring pan (which holds 7 cups of water).

Bake for 30 minutes, or until the sides start to shrink, the centre springs back when pressed, and a skewer comes out clean.

Leave for about 10 minutes before turning carefully out onto a rack. Cool to room temperature.

Serve sprinkled with a little icing sugar, and topped with whipped cream if you like.

# Lindsay's Apple & Walnut Cake

*Lindsay, a family friend, very kindly brought one of her apple cakes to Simon and Sam shortly after Isabella was born — it was so good that she then had to bring the recipe — here is our version of it! Enjoy it for dessert or with coffee.*

**For a 23cm ring (or 20cm round) cake:**
*125g butter*
*1 cup sugar*
*1 large egg*
*2 tsp mixed spice*
*1 tsp cinnamon*
*2 medium apples, chopped or sliced*
*1¼ cups flour*
*½ tsp baking soda*
*½ cup each chopped walnuts and sultanas*

Turn the oven to 190°C, or to 180°C if using a fan oven (see pages 6 and 7).

Melt the butter in a microwave bowl or pot. Remove from heat and add the sugar, egg and spices. Beat with a stirrer or fork until evenly mixed.

Chop the unpeeled apples into pieces about the size of sultanas or cut small cubes or slice apple quarters thinly with a sharp knife, or if you are using a food processor, slice chunky pieces from an apple into the processor, then chop in bursts with the metal chopping blade, repeating with the second apple. Stir into the butter mixture.

Measure the flour and soda into a sieve over the bowl or pot, shake in, add the chopped walnuts and sultanas, and fold everything together.

Thoroughly coat a 23cm ring tin or a 20cm round tin with non-stick spray, then spoon the cake mixture into it evenly.

Bake the ring cake for about 30 minutes, and the round cake for 35–45 minutes, until the centre springs back when pressed and a skewer in the centre comes out clean.

Serve warm dusted with icing sugar, plain, or with lightly whipped cream.

**VARIATION:** For a firmer, more substantial cake, to be eaten the day it is made, use 1½ cups flour instead of the smaller amount.

# Blueberry & Orange Coffee Cake

*Coffee cakes are another American "invention". Rather than being coffee flavoured, they are made to be eaten, preferably warm, with coffee. Make this one with fresh or (thawed) frozen blueberries at any time of the year.*

**For a 23cm round or square cake:**

**Topping:**

50g cold butter, cubed
½ cup sugar
⅓ cup flour
½ tsp cinnamon

**Cake:**

finely grated rind of 1 orange
¾ cup sugar
50g butter, softened
1 large egg
½ cup orange juice
¼ cup water
2 cups self-raising flour
½ tsp salt
1–2 cups fresh or thawed blueberries

Turn the oven to 180°C, or to 170°C if using a fan oven (see pages 6 and 7).

To make the topping, chop together the first four ingredients in a food processor (or rub them together by hand). Set aside the crumbly mixture while you make the cake.

For the cake, put grated orange rind and sugar in a large bowl or food processor.

Add the warmed, softened butter and the egg, then mix or process until combined.

Pour in the orange juice and water, without mixing. Measure the flour and salt into a sieve over the bowl, then shake them in. Mix until just blended.

Pour the batter into a 20 or 23cm square pan and sprinkle the blueberries evenly over the surface. Press them down gently, then sprinkle evenly with the topping.

Bake for about 45 minutes, or until a skewer comes out clean.

Cool slightly before cutting into squares.

Serve warm, dusted with icing sugar.

# Sour Cream Coffee Cake

*This cake is really easy to mix, and, if you add the filling and topping, it is really full of surprises!*

### For a 23cm ring cake:

1 (250g) carton sour cream

2 large eggs

1 cup sugar

1 tsp vanilla

1¾ cups self-raising flour

¼ tsp baking soda

½ tsp salt

### Topping (optional)

25g cold butter

¼ cup each sugar and chopped nuts

2 Tbsp flour

1 tsp cinnamon

### Filling (optional)

½ cup (50g) dried apricots

½ cup water

¼ cup each ground almonds, sugar and
    biscuit crumbs

Turn the oven to 180°C, or to 170°C if using a fan oven (see pages 6 and 7).

Line the bottom a 23cm ring tin (of 7 cup capacity) with baking paper and butter the sides or coat with non-stick spray.

Measure the sour cream, eggs, sugar and essence into a bowl or food processor.

Whisk or process until smooth, then sift in the flour, baking soda and salt and stir (or process briefly) to mix thoroughly but not more than necessary.

Pour mixture into the prepared pan.

To make the topping, cut or rub the butter into the remaining ingredients until it is crumbly.

To make the filling, finely chop the dried apricots, then boil them with the water for 3–4 minutes, until the water has disappeared. Cool apricots and mix with the ground almonds, sugar and biscuit crumbs.

Drop teaspoon lots of the (optional) filling over the surface of the uncooked cake, leaving the edges clear. (The filling sinks to the middle of the cake during cooking.) If using topping, sprinkle it evenly over the surface.

Bake for 40–45 minutes, until the thickest part of the cake springs back when pressed, and the edges start to shrink from the sides of the pan. Leave cake to stand in its tin for 10 minutes. Run a knife around the sides then invert carefully. Invert it again onto a plate and dust with icing sugar or leave plain.

Serve warm, with coffee, or with lightly whipped cream for dessert.

**VARIATION:** Replace apricot filling with spoonfuls of Christmas mincemeat or raspberry or apricot jam.

# Apricot & Cardamom Cake

*Cardamom gives this cake a particularly interesting flavour, but it may be left out, making a cake which is still delicious.*

**For a 23cm ring cake:**
*100g butter*
*¾ cup sugar*
*1 cup (half a 445g can) apricot pulp*
*finely grated rind of ½ lemon*
*1 tsp vanilla*
*1 tsp freshly ground cardamom*
*1 Tbsp lemon juice*
*2 large eggs*
*1 cup (130g) flour*
*⅔ cup (70g) ground almonds*
*1 tsp baking powder*
*½ tsp baking soda*
*¼–½ cup dried apricots, chopped small*

Turn the oven on to 190°C, or to 180°C if using a fan oven (see pages 6 and 7).

Spray a plain or fluted 23cm ring pan (with a 7 cup capacity) with non-stick spray. Sprinkle with flour, making sure all surfaces are coated, then bang pan to remove excess flour.

Heat the cubed butter gently in a large pot until melted. Remove from heat and add the sugar and unsweetened apricot pulp, then the next 5 ingredients in the order given. Beat with a fork or whisk until well combined.

Measure the flour, ground almonds, baking powder and soda into a large sieve over the pot. Shake into pot, then tip in any ground almonds remaining in the sieve. Sprinkle the dried apricots on top, then fold everything together, mixing until an even consistency, a little thinner than a butter-based cake mixture.

Pour batter into the prepared pan, then bake until centre feels firm and a skewer pushed to the bottom comes out clean, about 30–45 minutes.

Cool for 5 minutes, then carefully invert onto a cake rack. Dust with icing sugar before serving.

**VARIATION:** Leave out the cardamom if desired.

# Chocolate Zucchini Cake

*This delicious, moist, rich, chocolate-flavoured cake, has green flecks through it. The combination of ingredients seems unusual, but is most successful. The resulting cake is one of our favourites.*

**For a 23cm square cake:**
*125g butter*
*1 cup brown sugar*
*½ cup white sugar*
*3 large eggs*
*2½ cups flour*
*1 tsp vanilla*
*½ cup yoghurt*
*¼ cup cocoa*
*2 tsp baking soda*
*1 tsp cinnamon*
*½ tsp mixed spice*
*½ tsp salt*
*3 cups (350g) grated zucchini*
*½–1 cup chocolate chips*

Turn oven to 170°C, or to 160°C if using a fan oven (see pages 6 and 7).

Prepare a 23cm square pan by lining it with two crosswise strips of baking paper.

Beat the butter with the sugars until light and creamy using a food processor, mixer or stirrer. Do not hurry this step.

Add the eggs one at a time, with a spoonful of the measured flour to prevent the mixture from curdling. Add the vanilla and yoghurt and mix well.

Measure the remaining dry ingredients into a sieve over the bowl, and shake them in. Stir gently to partly combine with the egg mixture, then gently mix in the grated zucchini. Do not overmix.

Turn the mixture into the prepared tin and sprinkle the surface with the chocolate chips.

Bake for about 45 minutes, or until the centre feels firm and a skewer comes out clean.

Serve warm or cold, preferably within two days.

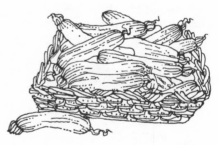

# Easy Fruit Cake

*This easily mixed cake is beautifully flavoured with fruit and nuts — no essences or spices are needed. It is unlikely to last long, but may be kept for weeks in a plastic bag in the refrigerator for instant snacks!*

**For a 23cm cake:**
*600g (4 cups) mixed fruit\**
*½ cup orange juice*
*200g butter*
*1 cup brown or white sugar*
*about 1 cup walnuts or other nuts*
*4 large eggs*
*1 cup self-raising flour*
*1 cup wholemeal or plain flour*

*\* Buy mixed fruit or use a mixture of sultanas, currants and Californian raisins*

Turn oven to 150°C, or to140°C if using a fan oven (see pages 6 and 7).

Simmer dried fruit and orange juice in a large covered pot for about 5 minutes or until all the juice is soaked up by the fruit, stirring every now and then.

Lift off the heat and stir in the butter, cut in 1cm cubes, and the sugar. (Pack brown sugar firmly into the cup.) Stir gently until butter melts and sugar loses its graininess, then stand pot in cold water to cool, stirring occasionally.

Chop the nuts roughly if they are in large pieces and stir them into the cooling mixture in the pot.

When cooled to room temperature, add the eggs, beating them in with a fork or a stirrer. When thoroughly mixed, sprinkle the flours over the mixture in the pot and stir everything together.

Pour mixture into a square 23cm tin lined with two strips of baking paper so the bottom and all sides are covered. Level the top.

Bake the cake at 150°C for 60–75 minutes, or until the centre feels firm and springs back when pressed and a skewer pushed into the middle (to the bottom) comes out clean. Cool in tin.

For best flavour, leave 2 days before cutting.

**VARIATIONS:** Make a deeper cake in a 20cm square tin. This will take longer to cook.

For a richer, festive cake use 1kg dried fruit and ¾ cup orange juice.

# Apricot & Almond Cake

*This is a cake for a special occasion! It tastes so good that you may well find yourself inventing special occasions so you can have another excuse to make it! Don't crush the biscuits too finely, or the cake will be too firm and dry.*

**For a 23cm round or ring cake:**
*140g slivered almonds*
*20 (75g) Snax biscuits*
*2 tsp baking powder*
*½ cup dried apricots, chopped*
*3 egg whites*
*1 cup sugar*
*1 tsp vanilla*

Turn oven to 180°C, or to 170°C if using a fan oven (see pages 6 and 7).

Toast the almonds lightly by heating them gently in a frying pan over low heat, or in a sponge roll pan under a grill. Do not let them get darker than straw colour. Put the nuts in a plastic bag with the biscuits. Bang the bag with a rolling pin until the biscuits are broken into small pieces but are not as fine as breadcrumbs. Add the baking powder and chopped apricots.

In a large, grease-free bowl, beat the egg whites until the peaks turn over. Add the sugar and beat again until the peaks stand up when the beater is removed. Fold in the vanilla.

Fold the crumb mixture into the meringue, then spoon the mixture into a ring tin which has been sprayed with non-stick spray, and has had its bottom lined with baking paper.

Bake for 30 minutes, then run a knife around the tin and carefully tip the cake out onto a rack.

As soon as the cake is cold, invert it again (so it is right way up!) onto a flat serving plate. Decorate with whipped cream, and garnish with more nuts or apricots.

Serve the day it is made.

# Date & Walnut Cake

*You can't actually see the fruit and nuts in this delicious cake because they are so finely chopped.*
*Serve it for dessert or for a special occasion, with coffee. (You need a food processor and beater to make it.)*

**For a 23cm round or ring cake:**
*1 cup (150g) chopped dates*
*1 cup (90g) walnut pieces*
*½ cup sugar*
*2 Tbsp flour*
*1 tsp baking powder*
*2 large eggs*
*1 tsp vanilla*

Turn oven to 180°C, or to 170°C if using a fan oven (see pages 6 and 7).

Line the bottom of a 23cm round cake tin with baking paper and spray sides with non-stick spray.

Measure the dates and nuts into a food processor. Add half of the measured sugar, all of the flour and baking powder, then chop until dates and nuts are as fine as rolled oats.

In another bowl beat the egg whites with half (2 Tbsp) of the remaining sugar until their peaks turn over when the beater is lifted from them. Beat egg yolks with the rest of sugar and vanilla until thick and creamy.

Combine the three mixtures, folding them together lightly, and turn mixture into the prepared tin.

Bake for about 30 minutes, until the centre springs back when pressed. Leave for 10 minutes then turn onto a rack to cool.

Serve topped with whipped cream, quark or ricotta, decorated with an interesting selection of chopped dried fruit and nuts, such as dates, dried apricots, walnuts and pecans.

NOTES: Use good quality dried fruit and nuts, especially walnuts.

This cake may be made ahead and frozen. It is best decorated within three hours of serving.

Do not expect a high cake. This cake is meant to be fairly flat!

# Lemon Square

*This square has a delicious lemon custard topping and is so popular that we thought we should include it so that owners of food processors and lemon trees could try it! Unless you have the processor, forget it — just turn the page quickly!*

**For 16–20 pieces:**

*Base:*

2 cups flour
½ cup icing sugar
150g cold butter

*Topping:*

1½ cups sugar
thinly peeled rind of ½ lemon
3 large eggs
¼ cup lemon juice
¼ cup self-raising flour

Turn on oven to 160°C. Press a large piece of baking paper into a 23cm square pan or a smallish sponge roll pan, folding the paper so it covers the bottom and all sides of the pan. Fold rather than cut the paper at the corners so filling cannot run underneath it.

Measure the flour, icing sugar and cubed butter into a food processor fitted with its metal chopping blade. Process until the butter is chopped finely through the dry ingredients. Tip mixture into the lined tin and press down firmly and evenly with the back of a large spoon or a fish slice.

Bake for 15–20 minutes or until firm and straw-coloured. While the base cooks, prepare the topping.

Put the sugar in the (unwashed) food processor with the rind peeled from half the lemon, using a potato peeler.

Process until the rind is very finely chopped through the sugar, then add the eggs, lemon juice, and flour. Process until smooth.

Pour on to the partly-cooked base, then bake for about 30 minutes longer, or until top is lightly browned and centre does not wobble when tin is jiggled.

When quite cold, cut into squares or fingers the size you like, by pressing a heavy, lightly oiled knife straight down through the topping and base.

Store, lightly covered, up to 3 or 4 days. Sift icing sugar over squares just before serving if you like.

# Cherry Slice

*This is a recipe I worked out after trying a delicious but expensive store bought slice in London. (It was so good, my sister and I ate our purchase before we left the store!) My version is quick (if you have a food processor) and a fraction of the price!*

**For about 16 pieces:**

**Base:**
1 cup flour
¼ cup sugar
100g cold butter

**Filling:**
¼–½ cup raspberry jam
¼–½ cup chopped crystallised cherries

**Topping:**
1½ cups medium or fine desiccated
    coconut
1 cup sugar
½ cup flour
½ cup flaked almonds, optional
50g cold butter
2 large eggs
¼ tsp almond essence

Turn the oven to 180°C. Spray a 23cm square tin with non-stick spray.

First make the base. Put the flour and sugar in the food processor bowl (with the metal chopping blade). Add the very cold butter, cut into about 9 small cubes. Process until the butter is cut into very small crumbs, then press the mixture into the prepared tin with the back of a fish slice or anything flat.

Bake the base for 15 minutes. While it bakes, prepare the filling and topping.

Chop the cherries fairly finely and put aside.

Combine the first four topping ingredients in the (unwashed) food processor bowl. Add the butter, cut into nine cubes, then process with the metal chopping blade until butter is cut through the mixture. Add the eggs and essence and blend until well mixed.

Take the partly cooked base from the oven. Spread it with the jam then sprinkle the cherries over it. Cover this with teaspoonfuls of the topping mixture, dropping this on with two spoons. Spread the topping lightly, so the jam and cherries are almost covered, trying to avoid mixing the two layers.

Bake at the same temperature for another 20–30 minutes, until the topping browns lightly and is firm when touched.

Leave to cool on a rack for 15 minutes before cutting carefully into squares or fingers. Pack pieces between layers of plastic in an airtight container.

Refrigerate up to a week or freeze for longer storage.

**VARIATION:** To make this without a food processor, melt the butter for the base and topping, and stir it into the remaining ingredients.

*Photograph shown on page 52.*

# Butterscotch Fingers

*Alison simplified an old favourite, three-layered butterscotch bar to make a recipe simple enough for her "Beginners" cookbook. The resulting bar tastes good anytime and may be hidden in the freezer for weeks.*

**About 20 slices, depending on size:**
*125g butter*
*½ cup sugar*
*1 large egg*
*1 tsp vanilla*
*1 cup self-raising flour*
*1 cup plain flour*

**Filling:**
*100g butter*
*2 rounded household tablespoons*
*   golden syrup*
*400g can sweetened condensed milk*

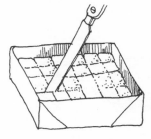

Turn the oven on to 180°C, and line a baking tin 23cm square or a small sponge roll tin with 2 strips of baking paper, so paper goes up all sides.

Cut butter in 9 pieces and warm in a large pot or microwave dish until starting to melt. Take off heat and beat in the sugar, egg and vanilla with a fork or stirrer, until evenly mixed.

Stir in the flours until mixture is crumbly, then squeeze it into a ball, using your hands. Break ¾ of the dough into bits, place these evenly in the prepared baking tin and pat them fairly flat, putting a piece of plastic between the mixture and your fingers if you like. Put the rest of the dough in the refrigerator or freezer.

To make the filling, melt the butter in a pot or microwave-proof bowl. Measure the syrup, using a hot wet spoon, and stir

in. Add the condensed milk, mix well, then pour over the unbaked mixture in the tin.

For the topping, coarsely grate the remaining (cold) piece of dough on top of the filling, using a grater with large holes.

Bake for 30–45 minutes, until the crust is golden and the filling has browned. (It may take a little longer in an oven without a fan.)

Leave for 2 hours, then remove from the baking tin and cut into pieces the size you like, using a sharp knife dipped in hot water.

Store in a covered container, refrigerating if keeping for a week or so, or freezing for longer storage.

Photograph shown on page 24.

# Coconut Slice

*This has been a family favourite for thirty years. Serve warm for dessert or cut in smaller pieces when cold, for a very popular slice. It is easy to make your own pastry in a food processor, but you can use bought pastry if you like.*

*About 8 servings:*

*Pastry\*:*
1 cup flour
75g cold butter
about ¼ cup cold water

*Filling:*
about ¼ cup raspberry jam
about ½ cup currants or sultanas

*Topping:*
175g butter
1½ cups sugar
1 tsp vanilla
3 large eggs
3 cups fine or medium coconut

*\* For an extra-easy version, replace the homemade pastry with 200g of bought sweet short pastry, or a sheet of prerolled flaky pastry, pricked all over before covering with filling.*

Heat the oven to 220°C, or to 210°C if using a fan oven (see pages 6 and 7). If using home-made pastry, make it first.

Put the flour and cubed butter in the food processor, then process in bursts, while adding the water in a slow stream. Stop as soon as you can press the dough particles together to make a firm dough.

Refrigerate dough 5–10 minutes while you mix the topping.

To make topping, soften but do not melt the butter, beat in the sugar, essence and eggs, then stir in the coconut.

Roll out the homemade or bought pastry to fit a 23cm square pan or a sponge roll tin, spread it with the jam and dried fruit, then drop the topping over it in blobs, spreading so most of the surface is covered. (Topping will spread during cooking.)

Bake for 10–15 minutes, then turn down to 180°C (170° for fan bake) and cook for 15–30 minutes or until the topping has browned evenly, and the centre feels firm.

Serve warm or cool in the tin before cutting into smaller pieces for a slice.

# Ginger Crunch

*Ginger crunch is another perennial family favourite. Even though it seems to have been around 'forever', it is still popular with nearly everybody we know, especially if we make a generous amount of icing!*

**For about 30 pieces:**

**Base:**

125g butter
¼ cup sugar
1 tsp baking powder
1 cup flour
1 tsp ground ginger

**Icing:**

2 Tbsp butter
2 tsp ground ginger
2 rounded household Tbsp golden syrup
1 Tbsp water
2 cups icing sugar

Heat the oven to 180°C, or to 170°C if using a fan oven (see pages 6 and 7).

Cut the cold butter into nine cubes, then process in brief bursts with remaining base ingredients, until the mixture is the texture of coarse breadcrumbs.

If mixing by hand, warm butter until soft, mix it with the sugar, then stir in the sieved dry ingredients.

Non-stick spray or line a 23cm square tin or a 20x30cm sponge roll tin with baking paper. Spread the crumbly mixture as evenly as possible into the tin and press it down firmly and evenly.

Bake for about 10 minutes or until evenly and lightly browned.  It will still feel soft while it is hot.

While the base cooks make the icing, since the base should be iced while hot.

Measure the butter, ginger, golden syrup and water into a small pot or microwave bowl.  Heat, without boiling, until melted.  Remove from the heat, sift in the icing sugar and beat until smooth.

As soon as the base is cooked, remove it from the oven. Pour the warm icing onto the hot base and spread carefully so it covers the base evenly.

Leave the square to cool and set, marking it into pieces while still warm. Do not remove from the tin until it has cooled completely.

**NOTE:** If you like a really thick icing, use one and a half times the icing recipe!

# Fudge Brownies

*Brownies are traditional American favourites. With their dense, fudgy and slightly chewy texture (and of course their delicious chocolate flavour!) they are becoming increasingly popular in New Zealand homes and cafes.*

**For about 24 pieces:**

*125g butter*
*1 cup sugar*
*2 large eggs*
*1 tsp vanilla*
*1 cup less 1 Tbsp flour (100g)*
*5 Tbsp cocoa*
*1 tsp baking powder*
*½ cup chopped walnuts, optional*

Turn oven to 180°C, or to 170°C if using a fan oven (see pages 6 and 7).

Mix the brownies in a medium-sized pot or microwave bowl. Melt the butter until it is liquid but not hot. Remove from the heat and beat in (using a fork or stirrer) the sugar, eggs, and vanilla.

Sift in the flour, cocoa and baking powder. Add the chopped nuts (if using) and stir until just combined — avoid over-mixing.

Pour mixture into a 20–23cm square tin lined with baking paper. Smooth the surface.

Bake for 30 minutes, or until firm in the centre. Mixture will rise up and sink again. The edges will probably be a little higher than the middle, but this does not matter. When cold, cut into rectangles.

Serve as is, dusted with icing sugar or rolled in sifted icing sugar, so all surfaces are covered, just before serving. Brownies do not require icing.

Great served as a snack with tea or coffee, or, with icecream for dessert.

# Boiled Fruit Loaf

*Alison started making this just after she was married, always following the instructions to slice after 24 hours. As years went by however, her loaves would vanish as after-school snacks and lunch box fillers, leaving only a few crumbs 24 hours later!*

**For a loaf about 10x23cm:**
1 cup water
¾ cup sugar
1 cup sultanas or dried fruit
25g (2 Tbsp) butter
1 tsp cinnamon
1 tsp mixed spice
½ tsp ground cloves
½ tsp salt
1½ cups flour
1 tsp baking powder
½ tsp baking soda

Turn the oven to 180°C, or to 170°C if using a fan oven (see pages 6 and 7).

Put the first eight ingredients into a medium-sized pot. Bring to the boil, stirring occasionally, then simmer gently, uncovered, for 5 minutes. Stand the pot in a sink of cold water and cool to room temperature, stirring now and then. (This step is important!)

While you wait, sift or thoroughly stir the remaining ingredients together, and line the long sides and the bottom of a loaf tin with a strip of baking paper.

When the mixture in the pot is cold, carefully stir in the mixed ingredients.

(Mix only enough to blend, since over-mixing causes the mixture to toughen and rise to a peak in the middle during cooking.)

Bake for 45–60 minutes, or until centre springs back when pressed and a skewer pushed into the centre comes out clean.

If you can, leave for 24 hours before cutting, so the loaf is firmer and easier to cut in thin slices. You may not, however, consider this essential!

# Coconut Loaf

*This easy-to-make loaf contains no butter or oil, but is, all the same, a moist loaf with a lovely flavour.*
*Eat it the day it is made as a cake, or warm as a dessert, and after this, butter the slices.*

**For a loaf about 10x23cm:**
*2 large eggs*
*1 tsp vanilla*
*¼ tsp almond essence*
*¼ tsp salt*
*1½ cups milk*
*1½ cups (135g) fine desiccated coconut*
*1½ cups sugar*
*2 cups self-raising flour*

Turn the oven to 170°C, or to 160°C if using a fan oven (see pages 6 and 7).

Line the bottom and the long sides of a loaf tin (which holds about 7 cups of water) with a strip of baking paper, and spray the ends with non-stick spray, or lightly butter them.

Break the eggs into a medium-size mixing bowl, add the essences and salt, then the milk, and beat with a fork until well combined. Measure the coconut, sugar and flour into another container and mix well. Add this to the egg mixture and mix gently with a fork, spoon or stirrer until combined, taking care not to overmix. Pour into the prepared tin.

(If you have a food processor, put all ingredients except the flour into it, then process to mix well. Add the flour and mix very briefly, just enough to dampen flour. Turn into tin as above.)

Bake for 40–60 minutes, until the centre feels firm and a skewer, pushed right down to the base, comes out clean. (If the loaf browns too fast, cover the top with a piece of paper or turn the oven down 10°.) Remove cooked loaf from the tin after 5 minutes, and cool on a rack. Serve the warm loaf the day it is made, for dessert, with fruit and whipped cream, or sliced, with coffee. After the first day, cut and butter thinner slices.

NOTE: Fine and medium desiccated coconut are available. Medium weighs less, so you should add an extra ¼ cup for this recipe.

# Lemon Loaf

*The crunchy, sweet-sour topping on this easy loaf makes it interesting and different. This is a particularly useful recipe for anyone with a lemon tree in their garden.*

**For a loaf about 10x23cm:**
125g butter
¾ cup sugar
finely grated rind of 1 large, or 2 small
    lemons
2 large eggs
½ cup milk
1½ cups flour
2 tsp baking powder
½ tsp salt
½ cup chopped walnuts, raisins or
    sultanas
juice of 1 large or 2 small lemons
¼ cup sugar

Turn oven to 180°C, or to 170°C if using a fan oven (see pages 6 and 7).

Melt the butter in a large bowl. Add the first measure of sugar, the finely grated lemon rind, the eggs and milk and mix together thoroughly, using a fork or stirrer.

Measure the next four ingredients into another bowl and mix well with a fork. Tip into the liquid mixture and fold together. (Take care not to mix more than needed or you will toughen the loaf.)

Spoon into a loaf tin about 23x10cm, which has had the bottom and two long sides lined with a sheet of baking paper.

Bake for 45–75 minutes, or until the sides of the loaf shrink from the tin and a skewer in the middle of the loaf comes out clean. Check at regular intervals to make sure loaf does not overcook.

As soon as you take the loaf from the oven, mix the lemon juice with the second measure of sugar and spoon or pour this over the top of the hot loaf. Leave in the tin for 3–4 minutes, then lift out and leave to cool on a rack. Slice when cold, and serve plain or buttered.

# *Index*

# Index

# Acknowledgements

*We would like to thank the firms who provided us with the following food and products.*

**ALISON'S CHOICE** Dried fruits, nuts, seeds, chocolate chips, ground almonds, etc.

**BENNICK'S POULTRY FARM,** Buller Rd. Levin, Fresh eggs

**CHEFMATE,** non-stick spray

**EMPIRE FOODSTUFFS,** Spices

**LUPI,** Olive oil and balsamic vinegar

**SUREBAKE,** Non-stick Teflon liners

**TARARUA,** Cultured dairy products

*The following firms kindly supplied the beautiful tableware photographed in this book.*

**THE LILY HOUSE,** Wellington
Coffee cups and plates, page 23 • Trug, page 42

**MEMORY LANE,** Wellington
Teacup, saucer and plate, page 41

**MOORE WILSON,** Wellington
Yellow cookie jar, page 13 • Plates, coffee maker and cup, page 24

**STEVENS,** Lower Hutt
Striped glasses and plates, page 13 • Glass bowl, page 23 • Cake stand and gold-rimmed wine glasses, page 51

**THEME,** Wellington
Gold-rimmed glass plate, cover • Glass bowl, page 14

# Knives

*For about 20 years I have imported my favourite, very sharp, kitchen knives from Switzerland. They keep their edges well, are easy to sharpen, a pleasure to use, and make excellent gifts.*

## VEGETABLE KNIFE $8.00

Ideal for cutting and peeling vegetables, these knives have a straight edged 85mm blade and black (dishwasher-proof) nylon handle. Each knife comes in an individual plastic sheath.

## BONING/UTILITY KNIFE $9.50

Excellent for boning chicken and other meats, and/or general kitchen duties. Featuring a 103mm blade that curves to a point and a dishwasher-proof, black nylon handle, each knife comes in a plastic sheath.

## SERRATED KNIFE $9.50

I find these knives unbelievably useful and I'm sure you will too! They are perfect for cutting cooked meats, ripe fruit and vegetables, and slicing bread and baking. Treated carefully, these blades stay sharp for years. The serrated 110mm blade is rounded at the end with a black (dishwasher-proof) nylon handle. Each knife comes in an individual plastic sheath.

## THREE-PIECE SET $20.00

This three-piece set includes a vegetable knife, a serrated knife (as described above) and a right-handed potato peeler with a matching black handle, presented in a white plastic wallet.

## GIFT BOXED KNIFE SET $44.00

This set contains five knives plus a matching right-handed potato peeler. There is a straight bladed vegetable knife and a serrated knife (as above), as well as a handy 85mm serrated blade vegetable knife, a small (85mm) utility knife with a pointed tip and a smaller (85mm) serrated knife. These elegantly presented sets make ideal gifts.

## SERRATED CARVING KNIFE $28.50

This fabulous knife cuts beautifully and is a pleasure to use. The 21cm serrated blade does not require sharpening. Once again the knife has a black moulded, dishwasher safe handle and comes in a plastic sheath.

## STEEL $20.00

The steel has 20cm blade and measures 33cm in total. With its matching black handle the steel is an ideal companion to your own knives, or as a gift. I have had excellent results using the steel. N.B. Not for use with serrated knives.

## PROBUS SPREADER/SCRAPER $6.50

After my knives, this is the most used tool in my kitchen! With a comfortable plastic handle, metal shank and flexible plastic blade (suitable for use on non-stick surfaces), these are excellent for mixing muffin batters, stirring and scraping bowls, spreading icings, turning pikelets, etc.

## NON-STICK TEFLON LINERS

I regard these SureBrand Teflon liners as another essential kitchen item. They really help avoid the frustration of stuck-on baking, roasting or frying. Once you've used them, you'll wonder how you did without!

| | |
|---|---|
| Round tin liner (for 15–23cm tins) | $6.50 |
| Round tin liner (for 23–30cm tins) | $9.50 |
| Square tin liner (for 15–23cm tins) | $6.50 |
| Square tin liner (for 23–30cm tins) | $9.50 |
| Ring tin liner (for 23cm tins) | $6.95 |
| Baking sheet liner (33 × 44cm) | $13.95 |

Prices as at 1 April 2005, all prices include GST. **Please add $3.50 post & packing to any knife/spreader order (any number of items). Please note, Teflon prices** <u>include</u> **post & packing.**

Make cheques payable to Alison Holst Mail Orders and post to:  Alison Holst Mail Orders
Freepost 124807
PO Box 17016
Wellington

Or, visit us at www.holst.co.nz